CHICKEN
SOUP

CHICKEN SOUP

38 INTERNATIONAL RECIPES FROM TRADITIONAL TO CONTEMPORARY

BY LINDA ZIMMERMAN

Illustrations by Sally Sturman

CLARKSON POTTER / PUBLISHERS
NEW YORK

*This one's for Bobby Littman
with love and gratitude*

Published by Clarkson N. Potter, Inc., 201 East 50th Street, New
York, New York 10022. Member of the Crown Publishing Group.
Random House, Inc. New York, Toronto, London,
Sydney, Auckland
CLARKSON N. POTTER, POTTER, and colophon are trade-
marks of Clarkson N. Potter, Inc.
Manufactured in the United States of America

Design by Lisa Plattner

Library of Congress Cataloging-in-Publication Data
Zimmerman, Linda.
Chicken soup: 38 international recipes from traditional to contempo-
rary/by Linda Zimmerman; illustrations by Sally Sturman.
Includes index.
1. Soups. 2. Cookery (Chicken) 3. Cookery, International.
I. Title
TX757.Z56 1994
641.8'13—dc20   93-19280 CIP
ISBN 0-517-58622-3

10 9 8 7 6 5 4 3 2 1
First Edition

CONTENTS

INTRODUCTION
7

CLEAR SOUPS
14

HEARTY SOUPS
32

ELEGANT CREAM SOUPS
70

ACCOMPANIMENTS AND CONDIMENTS
84

ACKNOWLEDGMENTS
94

INDEX
95

INTRODUCTION

A few years ago I saw a cartoon in *The New Yorker* depicting a little old lady bundled up in fur coat and galoshes, standing on a blustery street corner next to her "Hot Chicken Soup" pushcart, anxiously waiting to serve freezing passersby. It perfectly conjured up our universal image of chicken soup—the ultimate comfort food often referred to as "Jewish penicillin," but actually every mother's favorite remedy for what ails us.

Since antiquity, good cooks the world over have recognized the versatility of a pot of water, a chicken, and a few vegetables. Even Moses Maimonides, the brilliant twelfth-century Hebrew scholar, physician, and rabbi, recommended chicken soup as a remedy for "black humors." But the essence of this simple brew is more than a panacea. Chicken soup is delicious as well as nutritious. Whether called Cock-a-Leekie in Scotland, Caldo de Pollo in Mexico, Paeksuk in Korea, or Poulet au Pot in France, they are similar renditions of chicken soup and are loved by almost everyone.

During my research for this book, I was overwhelmed by the astounding number of soups that are based on rich chicken stock. I've assembled a wide variety of what I think are the best of the chicken soups I tested and tasted. Ranging from classic to contemporary, all have similar beginnings, yet very different and delectable endings.

Clear Soups offers a Basic Chicken Broth and two vari-

7

ations as well as a quick Pressure-Cooked Chicken Stock, which are the foundation for all the recipes in this book. You'll also find a never-fail Matzo Ball Soup, a delicate Italian Stracciatella (chicken broth served with a fluffy mixture of finely chopped fresh spinach, grated Parmesan cheese, and beaten egg), a tasty Scottish Cock-a-Leekie, sweetened with prunes, and an exotic Hawaiian Chicken and Green Papaya Soup.

Hearty Soups is filled with soups that are equally satisfying as either starters or heftier entrées that can be accompanied by a crisp salad and some good crusty bread. Chicken Tortilla Soup, with its cumin, chiles, and softened tortillas, and its garnish of avocado and cilantro, bursts with the flavors of Mexico and the Southwest; spicy Chicken and Sausage Gumbo is loaded with onions, bell peppers, chicken, and sausage and is almost more stew than soup; and *Pho Ga*, Vietnamese chicken noodle soup, is a complete meal in itself. For lighter but equally gratifying meals, you might want to try Escarole, Sun-dried Tomato, and Basmati Rice Chicken Soup, or Southwestern Chicken and Corn Dumpling Soup.

Elegant Cream Soups are appropriate for special occasions as well as family dinners. One of my favorites is the exotic Tom Ka Kai (hot and sour coconut milk soup with chicken and lime leaves from Thailand), but I also love to serve the lemony Greek Avgolemono Soup, which is delicious either hot or chilled.

Finally, *Accompaniments and Condiments* contains basic recipes such as Turkey Wontons, Fluffy Kasha, and Farina Dumplings that are not only delicious additions to soup, but are useful as well in any cook's repertoire.

Making Great Chicken Soup

Equipment It's not necessary to have a fancy *batterie de cuisine* to make great soup, but if you're planning on purchasing kitchen appliances, check out your local restaurant supply stores. You'll be able to acquire heavy-duty, good quality equipment at reasonable prices.

Pots The best kind of pot for making stock is one that distributes heat evenly and prevents scorching. Stock pots, which are tall and narrow, have sturdy handles on both sides and range in capacity from 4 to 22 quarts. Because these pots are tall and narrow, they prevent the liquid from evaporating too quickly. My favorites are All-Clad "Master-Chef" stockpots, which are made of heavy-gauge cast aluminum with stainless steel interiors.

Soup pots, Dutch ovens, large saucepans, kettles with lids, or even lobster pots and spaghetti cookers are equally fine for soup making as long as they're made of a heavy-gauge material, such as stainless steel or tin-lined copper or aluminum, or porcelain or enamel-coated cast iron.

Don't use an aluminum pot when cooking with acidic foods or making cream soups, unless the pot is lined with a nonreactive metal. Otherwise, cream or eggs will react to the metal and turn the soup an unappetizing gray.

Colanders Large colanders with curved, steel-riveted handles are useful for draining large quantities of stock. I also line them with cheesecloth to strain broth.

Double Mesh Hand-Held Strainers Hand strainers facilitate the removal of bits of food from the broth. These little work horses are made of two layers of tin-coated steel mesh, one fine and the other coarse. The strainers must be kept scrupulously clean, as food tends to wedge itself between the two layers of mesh, and they should be kept dry to prevent rusting around the rims. Sizes vary, but the 7½-inch strainer is the one I prefer.

Ladles Stainless steel ladles, with or without perforations, come in various sizes. The unperforated ladles are perfect for serving soup. Use the perforated ones to remove vegetables and meat from the broth.

Spoons Stainless steel spoons with 11-, 13-, or 15-inch handles make good tasting spoons. Long-handled wooden spoons are ideal for stirring as they don't conduct heat, react to the food, or scratch the pot. Perforated spoons are helpful to remove scum that rises to the top.

Skimmers Stainless steel fine mesh or perforated skimmers with long handles are useful for removing scum and excess fat from the surface of the soup.

Degreasing Cups Available in 1- or 4-cup sizes, these spouted cups facilitate the removal of fat from soup. After the cup is filled with soup, the fat rises to the top of the cup, leaving the defatted liquid to settle at the bottom of the cup. The defatted broth is poured out through the spout and the remaining fat is discarded.

Tongs Stainless steel utility spring tongs are perfect for fishing out bits of food from the broth. They're made in two weights—regular and heavy duty—and come in 10-, 12-, and 16-lengths.

Large Measuring Bowls Large bowls with lips and handles are perfect for when you're cooling or straining soups. I find the 3-quart stainless steel and 2-quart Pyrex types to be the most convenient.

Chicken Soup ABCs

There's no right or wrong to making the soups in this book as the recipes are very flexible. Use vegetables or herbs to taste, if you prefer. And if you don't have a particular herb or vegetable on hand, you can substitute another.

Chickens Years ago, stewing chickens (both roosters and hens that were past their prime) were the favorites of good cooks for the soup pot. After the soup simmered on top of the stove for several hours, all of the good chickeny essence of these tough birds was released into the soup.

Although the most commonly found chickens in the supermarket are roasters (4 pounds and up) and fryers (about 2½ to 4 pounds), soup or stewing chickens are still raised and sold, but they're fatter and more tender than the stewing chickens of the past. They range in size from 5 to 8 pounds, cost about half the price of a roasting chicken, and are sometimes even less expensive than fryers. If you can't find them in your supermarket, try a kosher or Chinese poultry shop, or even an Asian supermarket (these markets also sell chicken feet).

Regardless of type, the best chickens for soup are corn fed, minimally processed, and hormone and antibiotic free. They have deep yellow fat that not only turns the soup a beautiful golden color but also enhances the flavor.

If you can find chicken feet, always use them when cooking your soup. They, as well as the gizzards, produce a much more gelatinous soup, which gives it more body.

Delicious chicken broth can also be be made with the giblets (gizzards and hearts), backs, necks, wing tips, or any other part of the chicken (or trimmed bones, for that matter). If you make friends with a butcher, you can probably strike a deal with him or her to save for you any chicken odds and ends, which they usually discard when they trim the breasts. I always have a supply of trimmings in the freezer for an impromptu chicken soup.

Chilling the Broth Soup should be strained into a large bowl and allowed to cool at room temperature uncovered. Once it is cool, immediately refrigerate it, or freeze it in tightly covered containers to avoid any bacterial growth. Do not freeze or refrigerate hot stock.

Removing the Fat If you're using the broth immediately, degreasing cups and skimmers are the most efficient tools to defat. My favorites are the ones similar to measuring cups with a pouring spout (see page 10).

Chilling the broth for 6 to 8 hours allows the fat to congeal on the surface of the soup. Lift or scrape it off with a large spoon. The broth will be fat free but will still retain the intense chickeny flavor imparted by the fat.

Storage Store soup in an airtight container for up to 5 days in the refrigerator, or for 3 to 4 months in the freezer. Chicken soup or stock sours easily, so if you plan to keep it without freezing, bring the broth to a complete boil for 5 minutes after 2 to 3 days of refrigeration. Cool to room temperature uncovered and chill immediately.

Freezing Freeze soups in 1- or 2-cup containers. They should be filled about ⅔- to ¾-full (about 1 inch from the top) to allow for the liquid to expand. If you prefer to have small quantities of stock available for flavoring or stir-frying vegetables, freeze the stock in plastic-covered ice cube trays and pop out only the amount needed, or store the cubes in airtight plastic bags.

Thawing Allow frozen broth to defrost in the refrigerator overnight, or at room temperature. As soon as there is some liquid in the container, the frozen soup can be easily popped out into a heavy pot and melted frozen over low heat. If you need stock that has been frozen in a pinch, run hot water over the container or place it in a bowl of hot water until the stock around the edges has liquefied. Then pop out the frozen stock and heat as above.

Tips

Stock made only from bones should be cooked at least 3 to 5 hours for the most flavor to be released.

If you're making chicken soup with fryers and plan to use the meat, don't cook it for more than 2 hours, or the meat will fall apart and become tasteless.

Commercial-size cans of chicken broth (such as the 49½-ounce Swanson's Chicken Consomme) can be used to replace 6 cups of homemade stock. If using canned soup that is not low-sodium, taste it before adding salt.

Too many greens, such as leek tops, or herbs, will give a green cast to the soup. For a sweeter, deeper colored soup, add more parsnips or carrots. The color will also be deeper if you add an unpeeled yellow onion.

Chicken soup clouds if allowed to boil during cooking, so always simmer it over a low flame.

If you need to quickly strain the fat from chicken soup, strain it through a paper towel or cheesecloth several times.

Clear Soups

Basic Chicken Broth

Makes 8 to 10 cups

This broth is delicious with vegetables or noodles, or as the base for other soups. If you prefer a lighter flavor for vegetable-based soups, add more water to taste.

1	large stewing chicken or small roaster (about 4 pounds), quartered
1½	pounds chicken parts, such as backbones, wings, giblets, and feet
2½–3	quarts cold water
6	whole cloves
1	large onion, peeled
2	large carrots, peeled and halved
2	celery stalks, trimmed, leaving some leaves
1	large parsnip, peeled and halved
2	teaspoons black peppercorns
3	bay leaves
3	large sprigs fresh parsley
	Salt to taste
	Snipped fresh dill and parsley leaves

Wash all the chicken under cold water. Place in a large, heavy, deep soup pot that's not too wide, and cover with water (8 to 10 cups). Bring to a boil, lower heat, and simmer, uncovered, skimming the scum as it rises to the top. Continue simmering and skimming 30 to 45 minutes or until the broth is clear. Add 2 cups of cold water to bring additional scum to the surface and skim again until clear.

15

While the broth simmers, press the cloves into the onion. Add the onion, carrots, celery, parsnip, peppercorns, bay leaves, parsley sprigs, and salt to taste to the pot and simmer, partially covered, for 1½ hours.

Off the heat, let the broth cool slightly, then remove the chicken and vegetables, reserving them if you wish. Line a large strainer or colander with cheesecloth and strain the broth into a large bowl. Skim as much fat as possible off the surface with a degreaser cup, gravy strainer, or large spoon, or for use the following day, chill the broth overnight, and remove the congealed fat before reheating.

To serve, reheat the soup to simmering. Adjust salt to taste. Ladle into bowls and sprinkle with dill and parsley.

The broth can also be stored in the refrigerator for up to 5 days, or frozen in 1- or 2-cup containers (see page 12).

Note: For variety, try various root vegetables, in addition to carrots and parsnips, to flavor the soup. For a sweeter soup, add half of a red garnet sweet potato or yam.

Variations: ORIENTAL CHICKEN BROTH Replace the cloves, onion, carrots, celery, parsnip, bay leaves, parsley, and dill with one 3-inch piece of gingerroot that has been peeled and cut into 4 pieces, 2 scallions, 4 garlic cloves, and 1 teaspoon of Szechuan or black peppercorns.

ROASTED CHICKEN BROTH Replace the raw chicken with the bones of two roasted chickens, but use the same vegetables and seasonings as in Basic Chicken Broth. Simmer, partially covered, for 2 hours.

PRESSURE-COOKED CHICKEN STOCK

Makes 8 cups

Pressure cookers make rich-tasting stocks in less than half the time as traditional stove-top methods. Because there is little evaporation during the cooking process, the amount of stock made is usually equivalent to the amount of water used. Vary the flavor of the stock by using a variety of your favorite herbs. This recipe was tested on a cooker using 10 pounds of pressure.

4½	pounds chicken necks, backs, and gizzards
2	chicken feet (optional)
8	cups cold water
2	small leeks, trimmed, washed, and split lengthwise
2	medium carrots, scrubbed and cut into thirds
1	medium parsnip, scrubbed and cut into thirds
1	small turnip, peeled and halved
3	large celery stalks with leaves, halved
1	large onion, halved
6	whole cloves
2	sprigs fresh dill
10–12	sprigs fresh parsley
2	large bay leaves
1	tablespoon peppercorns, slightly crushed
	Salt to taste

Wash all the chicken parts under cold water. Place in a 6- to 8-quart pressure cooker with 8 cups of water. Slowly bring to almost boiling, skimming off the scum as it rises to the surface. When water is clear and free of scum, add the remaining ingredients.

Seal the cooker. Place the pressure regulator firmly on the vent pipe. When pressure regulator begins to gently rock, start timing. Cook for 30 minutes with pressure regulator rocking slowly and continuously, or follow the manufacturer's directions for your cooker.

Allow pressure to drop gradually with the lid in place until all the steam has left the cooker. Do not place the cooker under cold running water to reduce the pressure. Follow the manufacturer's directions for cooling. Cool the stock to room temperature, then strain through several layers of cheesecloth. Discard the vegetables, but reserve the chicken parts and gizzards for another use. Refrigerate the stock overnight for easy removal of excess fat.

STRACCIATELLA

Serves 4 to 6

This delicate soup from Rome takes minutes to make.

- 2 **large eggs**
- 3 **tablespoons grated Parmesan cheese**
- 1 **tablespoon semolina**
- 1 **tablespoon minced fresh parsley**
  Pinch of nutmeg
- 6 **cups Basic Chicken Broth (page 15)**
  Salt and freshly ground white pepper

In a small bowl, beat the eggs with the cheese, semolina, parsley, and nutmeg. Pour in 1 cup of broth and whisk until the mixture is well combined. Set aside.

Bring the remaining broth to a boil, then lower the heat. Whisk the egg mixture a few times and slowly pour into the simmering broth. Simmer about 5 minutes, whisking continuously. As the egg mixture cooks, it will break up into tiny flakes. When the soup is done, add salt and pepper to taste and serve immediately in individual bowls.

Variation: SPINACH-EGG SOUP Slice ½ pound of young spinach leaves into ¼-inch shreds. Rinse thoroughly, then dry in paper towels. Heat 2 teaspoons of olive oil in a large skillet. Sauté the spinach for 1 minute; set pan aside.

Just before the soup is done, remove spinach with a slotted spoon and stir into the soup. Simmer about 2 minutes, and serve.

MATZO BALL SOUP

Serves 4

The secret to light, fluffy matzo balls (also known as *knaidlach*) is in the handling. The ingredients should not be overmixed and the dumplings should be formed with a gentle touch to avoid compacting the mixture. I like to refrigerate the mixture overnight for an even tastier, more tender dumpling. This recipe will yield approximately 10 to 12 medium-large matzo balls.

3	large eggs
2½	tablespoons Rendered Chicken Fat (page 92), or vegetable oil
6	cups plus 3 tablespoons Basic Chicken Broth (page 15)
½	teaspoon ground nutmeg
¼	teaspoon white pepper
	Pinch of salt
⅔	cup matzo meal
8	cups water
¼	cup chopped fresh Italian parsley

In a medium bowl, beat together the eggs, chicken fat or oil, 3 tablespoons of the broth, nutmeg, white pepper, and salt. Add matzo meal and mix well with a fork until the mixture is completely incorporated and is thick and sticky. Cover the bowl and chill the mixture for at least 1 hour, until the matzo meal absorbs the liquid.

Place the water in a large pot and bring to a rolling boil.

Using a spoon, scoop small amounts of the matzo meal mixture and, with wet hands, gently form the mixture into 1½-inch balls. Drop one at a time into the boiling water. Lower the heat, cover, and simmer for 35 to 40 minutes without removing the lid. The matzo balls will double in size. Test one for doneness by cutting a matzo ball in half. The inside should be cooked through with no moist or doughy center.

Meanwhile, bring the remaining broth to a slow simmer in a large pot or saucepan. When the matzo balls are done, remove them from the water with a slotted spoon and add to the hot broth. To serve, adjust the seasonings, ladle the soup and matzo balls into bowls, and sprinkle with the parsley.

Note: Cooked matzo balls can be cooled, refrigerated overnight, and reheated in soup.

Variation: HERBED MATZO BALLS Reduce the nutmeg to ⅛ teaspoon and add 3 tablespoons chopped parsley, chives, dill, or cilantro to the ingredients, then proceed as above.

ZUPPA ALLA PAVESE
(CHICKEN SOUP WITH POACHED EGGS)

Serves 2

This well-loved soup is from Italy's Lombardy region. The eggs can be poached separately in plain water and then placed on the bread before adding the soup.

	Unsalted butter
2	½-inch-thick slices country French or rye bread
2¼	cups Basic Chicken Broth (page 15)
2	large eggs, at room temperature
¼	cup freshly grated Parmesan or Asiago cheese

Lightly butter the bread on both sides and brown in a frying pan, until crisp on the outside but soft inside. Place each slice in a soup bowl and keep warm in the oven.

Meanwhile, heat the soup to simmering, then lower the heat. Crack the eggs in two small dishes and slip the eggs into the simmering soup by tilting the cups one at a time. Poach until the whites are set and the yolks are a little runny, or to your desired doneness. Remove the bowls from the oven just before the eggs are done. Remove the eggs from the soup with a slotted spoon and place on top of the bread. Sprinkle with grated cheese. Divide the hot soup between the two bowls, pouring through a tea strainer. Serve immediately with more grated cheese, if desired.

TRICOLOR CHICKEN
SOUP WITH TORTELLINI

Serves 4 to 6

Tortellini in brodo (tortellini in broth) is a favorite first course for Sunday night dinner in the Emilia-Romagna region of Italy, where tortellini originated. I've added green peas, red bell peppers, and white-meat chicken to honor the colors of the Italian flag.

- 2 teaspoons olive oil
- 1 small red bell pepper, cut into ¼-inch dice
- 6 cups Basic Chicken Broth (page 15)
- 1 8- to 10-ounce package fresh spinach or chicken-filled tortellini, or a combination of both
- 1 cup cooked cubed chicken breast
- ½ cup fresh peas, or thawed frozen peas
- 2 tablespoons chopped fresh basil
  Salt and freshly ground pepper
  Grated Parmesan cheese (optional)

Heat the oil in a medium saucepan. Add the red bell pepper and sauté 2 minutes. Pour in the broth and heat to a simmer, then add the tortellini. Simmer uncovered, stirring occasionally, about 4 minutes, or until the pasta is *al dente*—just tender, but still firm. Add the chicken, peas, and basil. Simmer 1 or 2 more minutes. Season with salt and pepper to taste. Ladle into individual bowls and serve with a sprinkling of Parmesan cheese if you wish.

COCK-A-LEEKIE

Serves 4 to 6

This soup from Scotland combines the flavors of chicken and veal to create a rich broth. The prunes add a delicate hint of sweetness that marries well with the leeks. If you wish, you can thicken the soup by adding cream, barley, rice, or oatmeal.

1	4–5 pound capon or roasting chicken
1	pound veal neck bones
12	cups water
3	pounds leeks (10 to 12), trimmed leaving 2 inches of green
2	carrots, peeled and cut into thirds
2	bay leaves
1	teaspoon black peppercorns
½	teaspoon whole cloves
3	tablespoons unsalted butter
	Salt and white pepper
12	medium pitted prunes
	Chopped fresh parsley

Rinse the cavity of the chicken and remove any excess fat. Truss the chicken and place breast down with the veal bones in a very large Dutch oven or stock pot. Add the water and simmer, partially covered, for about 30 minutes, skimming the scum as it rises to the top of the pot.

Meanwhile, thinly slice half of the leeks (about 4½ cups), place in a colander, and thoroughly clean under cold running water. Set aside. Cut the remaining leeks in half, clean under cold running water, and add them to the pot along with the carrots, bay leaves, peppercorns, and cloves, making sure the surface of the soup has been thoroughly skimmed. Gently simmer, partially covered, for 1½ hours, or until the chicken is tender and falls from the bone.

Remove the chicken and veal from the pot and let cool. Pick any meat off the veal bones, and discard the bones. Remove the chicken meat, discarding the skin and bones. Cut the chicken into bite-size pieces and reserve. Strain the broth and discard the vegetables and spices. Skim any fat off the top or chill overnight and skim.

In a large heavy pot, melt the butter over medium heat. Add the reserved sliced leeks and season with salt and white pepper to taste. Sauté a few minutes, then cover and cook about 10 minutes, or until the leeks are translucent. Pour in the broth, bring to a simmer, lower the heat, and add the prunes. Simmer about 15 minutes. Add the chicken and veal. Simmer 10 more minutes or until heated through.

Ladle into bowls and sprinkle with parsley.

CHICKEN AND GREEN PAPAYA SOUP

Serves 4 to 6

This recipe is based on one created by "Henry Clay" Richardson when he was executive chef at the Kapalua Bay Hotel and Villas in Maui, Hawaii.

1	1½–2 ounce piece fresh gingerroot
2	tablespoons vegetable oil
2	pounds chicken parts, white and dark meat
3	garlic cloves
1½	tablespoons *nam pla*, or salt to taste
	Freshly ground black pepper
8	cups Basic Chicken Broth (page 15)
1	medium green papaya
30–40	fresh cilantro leaves

Peel the gingerroot, cut off a thumb-size piece, and reserve. Slice the remaining gingerroot into quarter-size pieces. Heat the oil in a large saucepan and add the sliced ginger, chicken, garlic, and *nam pla*. Lightly brown the chicken on all sides over medium-high heat, then pour off the fat. Season with pepper. Add the broth and bring to a simmer over medium heat. Lower the heat and simmer, skimming off any foam. Continue to simmer, partially covered, about 30 minutes, or until the chicken is tender. Remove the chicken and allow to cool.

Skim the fat from the soup, or chill the soup and then

remove the fat. Remove the chicken from the bones and cut into bite-size pieces. Peel, seed, and quarter the papaya and slice crosswise into ¼-inch pieces. Reheat the soup to simmering. Add the papaya, chicken, and cilantro, reserving a few leaves. Simmer 3 to 5 minutes, or until the papaya is tender, but maintains its shape. Grate the remaining ginger. Ladle the soup into bowls and sprinkle with a few cilantro leaves and a bit of grated ginger.

CHESHIRE
CHICKEN SOUP

Serves 3 to 4

This simple soup is so good on a rainy day.

4¼	cups Basic Chicken Broth (page 15)
1	cup chopped leeks, white part only
½	cup diced potato
¼	cup grated carrot
¼	cup uncooked regular oatmeal
1½	ounces Cheshire cheese, grated

Place the broth, leeks, and potato in a medium pot. Bring to just a boil, lower heat and simmer partially covered 15 minutes. Add the carrots. Stir in the oatmeal and simmer partially covered another 10 minutes. Serve immediately, topped with grated cheese.

CHINESE CHICKEN NOODLE SOUP

Serves 4 to 6

This main-dish soup can be quickly assembled if all the ingredients have been prepared in advance.

6	medium black Chinese or shiitake mushrooms, tough stems removed
½	cup warm water
1	pound fresh Chinese noodles, or any good egg noodles
	Peanut oil
8	cups Oriental Chicken Broth (page 16) or Basic Chicken Broth (page 15)
1	tablespoon Chinese rice wine or dry sherry
1	tablespoon dark Oriental sesame oil
1	tablespoon light soy sauce
¾	cup Chinese snow peas, cut into strips
1	small bunch Chinese broccoli (*gai lohn*), sliced into small pieces, or ¾ cup broccoli florets
2	baby bok choys, or ½ small bok choy, cut into pieces
½	pound barbecued, roasted, or cooked chicken, diced
½	pound medium shrimp, uncooked and shelled
3	scallions, trimmed and thinly sliced on an angle, green and white parts

Soak the mushrooms in the warm water for about 30 minutes. Rinse, dry, cut into slivers, and set aside.

Meanwhile, cook the noodles in a large pot of salted, boiling water according to package directions, just until firm, but not mushy. Drain in a colander, rinse under cold water, and separate with a fork. Toss with a little peanut oil to keep them from sticking together, and set aside.

Heat the chicken broth, rice wine, sesame oil, and soy sauce in a large pot to simmering, lower heat, and keep hot.

Heat a small amount of peanut oil in a wok or frying pan. Quickly sauté the snow peas, broccoli, and bok choy for about 1 minute. Remove the vegetables from the pan and set aside. Add the bok choy, mushrooms, chicken, and shrimp to the broth. Cook about 2 minutes or until shrimp are firm and pink and the chicken is heated through. Turn off heat. Add the snow peas and broccoli and stir to warm.

Just before serving, run the noodles under hot water to warm, shake to drain, then place equal portions in serving bowls. Ladle the soup, mushrooms, chicken, and shrimp on top of the noodles. Circle the top of each bowl with the vegetables and top each portion with sliced scallions. Serve immediately.

Note: The noodles can also be reheated in the pot with the chicken, shrimp, and mushrooms.

ORIENTAL SOUP NOODLE LUNCH FOR ONE

Serves 1

Instant Udon soup noodles are found in the refrigerator section of most large supermarkets. I love their convenience but find the packaged soup base too salty. If you use your homemade broth seasoned with miso (soybean paste) plus a variety of any vegetables on hand, you can throw together a quick, delicious, and inexpensive lunch without much work. You can easily double or triple this recipe.

1½ cups Oriental Chicken Broth (page 16) or Basic Chicken Broth (page 15)

1 large Brussels sprout, halved vertically and finely sliced

1 small carrot, scrubbed, peeled, and very thinly sliced on an angle

3 thin asparagus stalks, thinly sliced on an angle to the tip

1 scallion, green and white parts, trimmed and thinly sliced on an angle

½ cup diced ripe tomato

1½ teaspoons dark miso

1 7-ounce package fresh instant Udon noodles

Place broth, vegetables, and miso in a medium saucepan. Cover and bring to almost boiling. Add the noodles. Bring to almost boiling, lower the heat, and simmer 3 to 5 minutes. Stir the soup with chopsticks or a fork after 1 minute to prevent the noodles from sticking. Serve in a deep bowl.

WONTON SOUP

Serves 4 to 6

For a more substantial soup, any thinly sliced vegetables, such as carrots, mushrooms, or cabbage, can be added along with the bok choy.

6	cups Oriental Chicken Broth (page 16)
¼	cup rice wine
1	teaspoon dark Oriental sesame oil
1	tablespoon light soy sauce
1	large bok choy leaf, sliced on an angle
20–30	Turkey Wontons (page 85), cooked
2	scallions, green and white parts, thinly sliced

In a medium pot, combine the broth, rice wine, sesame oil, and soy sauce. Heat to simmering, then add the bok choy and wontons. Continue to simmer until the bok choy is just crisp and the wontons are just heated through, about 3 to 4 minutes. Ladle into heated bowls and sprinkle with the scallions.

HEARTY SOUPS

CHICKEN AND CORN DUMPLING SOUP

Serves 8 to 10

This colorful soup is based on a recipe from Chef Stephen Pyles of Dallas, Texas. The soup has an interesting contrast of flavors—spicy with a hint of sweetness. Serve it topped with Crème Fraîche or Crema Mexicana, a heavy cultured cream that can be found in Latin American markets.

2 tablespoons olive oil
6 scallions, white and green parts, thinly sliced
3 garlic cloves, minced
1 carrot, peeled and diced
1 medium yellow onion, peeled and diced
1 yellow bell pepper, seeded and diced
1 red bell pepper, seeded and diced
5 tomatillos, husked, rinsed, and diced
2 poblano chiles, roasted, peeled, seeded, and
      diced (see roasting directions, page 35)
2 medium-ripe tomatoes, blanched, peeled,
      seeded, and diced
8 cups Basic Chicken Broth (page 15)
1 tablespoon chopped fresh basil
1 tablespoon chopped fresh tarragon

CORN DUMPLINGS

1	cup water
4	tablespoons unsalted butter
2	teaspoons salt
1	cup sifted all-purpose flour
¾	cup fresh or thawed frozen corn kernels
4	large eggs
¼	cup chopped fresh chives
	Salt and freshly ground black pepper
4	cups shredded or cubed cooked chicken
8–10	tablespoons Crema Mexicana or Crème Fraîche (page 93)

Heat the oil in a Dutch oven or large (3- to 4-quart) heavy saucepan over medium heat. Sauté the scallions, garlic, carrot, onion, and bell peppers for 2 minutes. Add the tomatillos, poblanos, tomatoes, and broth. Bring to a boil, lower the heat, and add the herbs. Simmer, partially covered, for 20 minutes.

Meanwhile, prepare the dumplings. In a small saucepan, bring the water, butter, and salt to a boil. Slowly beat in the flour with a wooden spoon until the mixture is incorporated, pulls away from the pan, and no longer clings to the spoon, or use a whisk to incorporate and then beat with the spoon. Beat in the corn, and cook 1 minute longer. Remove from the heat and beat in the eggs, one at a time. Mix to thoroughly combine, then fold in the chives. Season with salt and pepper.

Separate the dough into tablespoon-size pieces and form into dumplings. Drop one at a time into the simmering soup. Cover and cook over low heat about 3 minutes, or until the dumplings are no longer doughy. Add the chicken to the soup, cover, and simmer for 3 to 5 minutes.

Ladle the hot soup and dumplings into individual bowls and top with a tablespoon of Crema Mexicana or a dollop of Crème Fraîche.

To Roast Chiles: Roast the chiles over very hot coals or over a high flame on top of the stove until blackened, turning with long tongs as they char. Remove from the heat and place in a paper or plastic bag, seal, and let steam 10 to 15 minutes. Peel off the charred skin with your fingers or scrape off with a sharp paring knife. Remove the seeds before cutting or dicing.

Note: Be careful not to touch your mouth or eyes when handling fresh chiles, as the hot oils found in their veins can cause painful burning or intense discomfort. It is advisable to wear disposable rubber gloves to protect your hands when working with any chiles.

HOT AND SOUR SOUP

Serves 6 to 8

This piquant but delicate soup is easy to make. For variety, try using fresh shiitakes and Chinese broccoli and replacing the chicken with pork, veal, or shrimp. Tree ears and tiger lily buds can be found at Asian markets.

16	dried tiger lily buds (golden needles)
5	large dried shiitake or black Chinese mushrooms
3	large dried tree ears (black cloud fungus)
¼	cup cornstarch
3	tablespoons light soy sauce
1	tablespoon dark Oriental sesame oil
1	teaspoon Chinese rice wine (*shaoxing*), or dry sherry
1	large skinless and boneless chicken breast, partially frozen
1	large egg, lightly beaten
6	cups Oriental Chicken Broth (page 16)
¼	cup thinly sliced bamboo shoots
3	tablespoons rice vinegar
1½	teaspoons freshly ground black pepper
1	10-ounce package fresh firm white tofu, drained and cubed
2	scallions, green and white parts, cut into ½-inch pieces
2	tablespoons chopped fresh cilantro

Place the tiger lily buds, shiitakes, and tree ears in three separate bowls. Cover each with boiling water and soak for at least 20 to 30 minutes. When soft, drain, rinse, and dry each. Cut off and discard the rounded end of the tiger lily buds and slice the buds in half lengthwise. Cut off and discard the woody ends of the shiitakes. Slice the shiitakes and tree ears into narrow strips.

In a small bowl, combine 1 tablespoon of cornstarch, 1 tablespoon soy sauce, 1 teaspoon sesame oil, and the rice wine with 1 teaspoon water. Slice the chicken into strips and toss with the cornstarch mixture to completely coat. Cover and marinate at room temperature for ½ hour.

When ready to make the soup, dissolve the remaining cornstarch in ¼ cup water, and reserve. In a separate cup, beat the egg with 1 teaspoon of the sesame oil and reserve.

In a large saucepan or heavy pot, bring the broth almost to boiling over high heat. Lower the heat, remove the chicken from the marinade, and stir into the broth, stirring continuously for 5 minutes. Stir in the lily buds, shiitakes, tree ears, and bamboo shoots. Stir in the remaining soy sauce, vinegar, and black pepper or cayenne. Stir the reserved cornstarch mixture, and add to the soup, stirring constantly to thicken, about 30 seconds. Add the tofu and simmer about 1 minute. Remove from the heat. Pour the egg mixture into the soup in a slow circular stream, stirring constantly so the egg will break into flakes. Stir in the remaining sesame oil. Adjust the vinegar and pepper to taste for a more piquant soup. Ladle into a hot tureen or warmed bowls and garnish with scallions and cilantro.

CHICKEN AND ONION
SOUP PROVENÇAL

Serves 4

This not-quite-traditional onion soup combines chunks of white-meat chicken with the flavors of the south of France.

10	garlic cloves, peeled
1	tablespoon unsalted butter
	Olive oil
1½	pounds sweet white onions, such as Walla Walla or Maui, thinly sliced
1	teaspoon dried thyme leaves
1	cup canned crushed tomatoes
1	bay leaf
6	cups Basic Chicken Broth (page 15)
1½	cups cubed cooked chicken breast
	Salt and freshly ground pepper
4	½-inch-thick slices seedless country rye or white bread
2	cups (about 8 ounces) grated Asiago, Swiss, Fontina, or any creamy hard cheese

Thinly slice 8 garlic cloves. In a 4- or 5-quart Dutch oven, melt the butter with 3 tablespoons of olive oil. Add the garlic, onions, and thyme. Sauté over medium heat, stirring to evenly coat the vegetables with oil. Turn the heat to medium low, cover the pot, and cook the vegetables for 10 minutes. Remove the lid and cook, stirring occasionally, for 10 more minutes. The volume of the vegetables will be greatly reduced. Stir in the tomatoes. Cook uncovered, stirring occasionally, for 25 minutes, or until the onions and tomatoes have turned a light golden red-brown. Add the bay leaf and chicken broth. Raise heat to bring the soup to a boil, then lower the heat and simmer, partially covered, for 35 to 40 minutes. Add the chicken, and cook 1 or 2 more minutes to heat through. Remove from the heat and season with salt and pepper to taste.

Preheat the oven to 350° F.

Lightly brush both sides of the bread slices with olive oil and lightly toast on a baking pan in the oven, about 10 to 15 minutes. The bread should be crisp on the outside and soft inside. (The bread can be toasted up to 2 days in advance and kept in an airtight container.) Crush the remaining garlic cloves and rub one side of the toast with the garlic.

Turn the oven to broil. Place each slice of bread, garlic side up, in a heat-resistant bowl or crock. Remove the bay leaf from the soup. Ladle the hot soup over the bread and sprinkle generously with the cheese. Place under the broiler 1 to 3 minutes, until the cheese is bubbly and just beginning to brown. Serve immediately.

Minestrone with Smoked Chicken

Serves 6 to 8

A colorful and seasonal minestrone can be made with a combination of your favorite vegetables and cooked beans throughout the year. This main-course dish is hearty but not heavy. The pesto should not be stirred in as the soup is eaten, or the soup will become cloudy.

¼	cup olive oil
1	onion, chopped
1	leek, white only, split vertically and sliced
¼	cup minced Italian parsley
4	ounces smoked chicken or turkey breast, diced
1	celery stalk, trimmed of leaves and chopped
2	carrots, peeled and chopped
1	bunch (about 4 leaves) white Swiss chard, cut into strips
½	small Savoy cabbage, or ½ small green cabbage, shredded
1	large potato, peeled and cubed
2	medium zucchini, vertically quartered and cut into slices
1	16-ounce can Italian-style plum tomatoes, drained, seeded, and chopped

1	cup canned cannellini or other white beans, plus ⅓ cup bean liquid
¼	pound fresh or frozen and thawed green beans, cut into 1-inch pieces
4–5	cups Basic Chicken Broth (page 15)
⅓	cup orzo, pastina, or other small pasta
	Salt and freshly ground pepper
¼	cup Pesto (page 89)
	Freshly grated Parmesan cheese

Heat the oil in a large saucepan over medium-low heat. Add the onion, leek, and parsley and sauté until the onions are wilted, about 10 minutes. Add half of the chicken, then the celery and carrots. Cook over medium heat for about 5 minutes, stirring occasionally. Add the Swiss chard and cabbage. Cook, stirring, until the Swiss chard and cabbage lose volume, about 5 minutes. Add the potato, zucchini, tomatoes, cannellini beans and liquid, green beans, and broth. Simmer over low heat, partially covered, for 30 to 35 minutes.

Meanwhile, cook the orzo about 8 to 10 minutes, or just until tender, then drain. (If holding the pasta aside, toss with a little oil to keep it from sticking together.) Five minutes before the soup is finished, stir the orzo and remaining chicken into the soup. Season with salt and pepper to taste. This is a thick soup, but it can be thinned with additional broth if desired.

Ladle the soup into individual bowls. Top with a dollop of Pesto. Serve with grated cheese on the side.

YUCATECAN CHICKEN-LIME SOUP

Serves 6 to 8

It's important to add the tortilla strips to the soup as quickly as possible after frying so they will crackle and sizzle when added to the hot broth. If you prefer, add 5 or 6 cooked chopped chicken livers to the soup, as they do in Mexico.

3	sprigs fresh oregano
1	head garlic, cloves separated but not peeled
½	pound chicken gizzards (about 10)
8	cups Basic Chicken Broth (page 15)
1	large whole chicken breast, split
4	medium white onions
10	whole allspice
4¼	cups corn oil
1	tablespoon chopped garlic
1	large onion, chopped
½	red bell pepper, seeded and diced
3	serrano chiles, seeded and minced
2	tomatoes, peeled, seeded, and chopped
	Salt and freshly ground pepper
1	lime, halved
12	corn tortillas, cut into ¼-inch strips
¼	cup freshly grated lime zest

In a small skillet, toast the oregano over medium-high heat for 1 minute, or just until crisp. Remove from the pan and set aside. Add the garlic cloves to the pan and toast for 3 to 5 minutes, turning to brown on all sides. Reserve.

Place the gizzards and broth in a large pot or Dutch oven. Simmer partially covered for 15 to 20 minutes, skimming as necessary. Add the chicken breast, oregano, garlic cloves, 2 white onions, and allspice. Simmer partially covered, skimming as necessary, for 20 to 30 minutes, or until the chicken is tender. Remove the chicken with a slotted spoon. When it is cool enough to handle, remove the skin and bones and discard. Shred the meat and set aside. Continue cooking the broth, about 30 to 40 minutes, or until the gizzards are tender. It may be necessary to add more water to the pot if the gizzards are tough and take a long time to cook. Strain the broth, discarding the vegetables and spices and retaining the gizzards. Chop the gizzards into small pieces and set aside.

Meanwhile, in a deep, heavy skillet or pan, heat 3 to 4 tablespoons of the oil. Add the chopped garlic and onion to the pan. Sauté for 5 minutes, then add the red bell pepper, ¼ teaspoon of the chopped chiles, and the tomatoes. Season with salt and pepper to taste. Cook over medium heat about 15 minutes, stirring while the mixture thickens. Add to the broth, then add the reserved chicken and gizzards. Bring to a simmer, and cook about 5 minutes. Squeeze in the juice from the lime halves, then add the rind to the pot. Cook 1 minute more and remove the lime rinds. Chop the remaining 2 white onions and set aside. Keep the soup warm while frying the tortilla strips.

Pour the remaining oil (about 1 inch in depth) into a

cast iron or heavy 10-inch skillet and heat to almost smoking. Fry the tortilla strips in small batches, turning often with long tongs or a long slotted spoon, for 30 to 40 seconds or just until crisp and lightly browned. Drain on paper towels.

Ladle the soup into individual bowls and add the hot tortilla strips. Serve the grated lime zest and the remaining chiles and chopped onions on the side.

SOPA DE FIDEOS
(MEXICAN-STYLE CHICKEN NOODLE SOUP WITH GARLIC SAUCE)

Serves 4 to 6

This comforting dish is really more noodles than soup. It's considered a dry soup in Mexico, because of the lack of liquid. The noodles are cooked similarly to Italian risotto.

- ¼ cup vegetable oil
- 2 Roma (Italian) tomatoes, chopped
- 2 garlic cloves, minced
- 1 small white onion, chopped
- 8 cups Basic Chicken Broth (page 15)
- 8 ounces fideos, vermicelli, or fine egg noodles, broken into 1-inch pieces
- ½ cup coarsely chopped fresh cilantro leaves
- 2–3 jalapeño or serrano chiles, seeded and minced
  Garlic Sauce (recipe follows)

Heat 2 tablespoons of the oil in a heavy saucepan over medium heat. Add the tomatoes, garlic, and onion and sauté for 10 minutes, or until the onion is soft and translucent. Pour the broth over the vegetables and simmer, partially covered, for 30 minutes.

Meanwhile, heat the remaining oil in a large skillet. Add the noodles and toast over medium-high heat, 5 to 8 minutes, or until light brown. Watch carefully so the noodles don't burn. This can be done in two batches.

Place the noodles in a heavy saucepan. Strain the broth and pour ½ cup over the noodles. Cook 10 minutes, until the noodles are soft and plump. Add the remaining soup and cook another 5 minutes, or until soup is hot and thick. Ladle into bowls and top with cilantro, chiles, and a dollop of Garlic Sauce. Serve immediately.

GARLIC SAUCE

Makes ½ cup

- 6 **cloves garlic**
- ½ **teaspoon salt**
- 2 **large egg yolks, at room temperature**
- 1 **teaspoon strained fresh lemon juice**
- ½ **cup mild olive oil**

Place the garlic, salt, egg yolks, and lemon juice in a blender. Blend on high speed until mixture is smooth, then slowly add the oil in a very thin stream until it is absorbed and forms an emulsion. Adjust salt to taste. Serve immediately or cover and refrigerate until ready to use.

Chicken Tortilla Soup

Serves 12

This soup became popular throughout the Southwest in the mid-1980s after being refined by chef Joe Venezia, who at that time headed the kitchen of the Bel Air Hotel in Bel Air, California. Pureed corn tortillas add an intriguing texture and somewhat nutty flavor.

15	corn tortillas
5	cups corn oil
¼	cup ground cumin
2	serrano chiles, seeded and minced
1	head garlic, cloves separated and chopped (about ⅓ cup)
1½	pounds tomatoes, peeled, seeded, and chopped
4	cups chopped onion
12	cups Basic Chicken Broth (page 15)
1	5-pound cooked chicken, skinned, boned, and meat shredded
	Salt and freshly ground pepper

GARNISH

3	avocados, peeled and cut into ¼-inch cubes
½	cup fresh cilantro leaves
1	pasilla chile, roasted, seeded, and cut into thin strips (see roasting directions, page 35)

1   Anaheim chile, roasted, seeded, and cut
    into thin strips (see roasting directions,
    page 35)
1   pound crumbled ranchero cheese or *queso
    fresco*, or shredded or cubed Jack or
    Cheddar cheese
2   cups sour cream
4   limes, cut into wedges

Tear 5 tortillas into small pieces. Heat 1 cup of corn oil in a Dutch oven or heavy saucepan. Cook the tortillas over medium-high heat for 1 minute or until soft. Add the cumin, chiles, garlic, tomatoes, and onion and cook for 10 minutes. Add the broth, lower the heat, and simmer, covered, for 20 to 30 minutes.

Ladle the soup in small batches into a blender and puree until smooth. Continue to puree in small batches. Strain and discard any solids. Return the soup to the pot. Add the chicken. Season to taste with salt and pepper. Reheat and keep warm.

Just before serving, cut the remaining tortillas into ¼-inch strips. Cut the strips in half. In a cast iron or heavy 10-inch skillet, heat the remaining oil to almost smoking. Fry the tortillas in small batches, turning frequently with long tongs, 30 to 40 seconds, or just until crisp and lightly browned. Drain on paper towels.

To serve, ladle the hot soup into individual bowls. Garnish with the fried tortilla strips, avocados, cilantro, chiles, cheese, sour cream, and lime wedges.

CHICKEN ALBONDIGAS SOUP

Serves 4 to 6

A friend created this soup for an informal dinner party years ago, and I've been making it ever since. The *albondigas* (meatballs) can be prepared a day or two ahead and reheated.

ALBONDIGAS (CHICKEN MEATBALLS)

1   **pound ground chicken or turkey**
½   **cup seasoned dry bread crumbs**
1   **large egg, lightly beaten**
¼   **cup coarsely chopped fresh cilantro leaves**
1   **teaspoon ground cumin**
¼   **teaspoon freshly ground white pepper**
    Salt
2–3   **tablespoons vegetable oil**

SOUP

2   **tablespoons vegetable oil**
½   **cup white rice**
2   **garlic cloves, minced**
2   **celery stalks with leaves, coarsely chopped**
2   **large onions, coarsely chopped**
6   **Roma (Italian plum) tomatoes (about ¾ pound), seeded, peeled, and pureed**
2   **large carrots, peeled and shredded**

1 **small cabbage (about 1 pound), cored and chopped**
5 **cups Basic Chicken Broth (page 15)**
1 **cup Spicy V8 Juice or any spicy tomato-vegetable juice**
2 **teaspoons ground cumin**
¼ **teaspoon cayenne**
Salt
Crème Fraîche (page 93) or sour cream

To make the *albondigas*, in a large bowl combine the chicken, bread crumbs, egg, cilantro, cumin, pepper, and a pinch of salt. Mix well with your hands. Lightly shape into 1-inch meatballs, packing lightly.

In a large, heavy skillet, heat the oil to sizzling. Sauté the meatballs in small batches until evenly browned. Drain on paper towels and reserve.

To make the soup, heat the oil in a large skillet until hot. Add the rice and sauté about 30 seconds, stirring to coat all the grains. Add the garlic, celery, and onion and sauté until the onion is translucent. Transfer to a Dutch oven or large pot. Add the tomatoes, carrots, cabbage, broth, juice, cumin, cayenne, and salt to taste. Simmer for 45 minutes, partially covered, or until the vegetables are cooked.

Add the *albondigas* a few at a time. Simmer an additional 5 minutes to heat through.

Adjust the salt, pepper, and cayenne to taste. Ladle into serving bowls and top with a dollop of Crème Fraîche or sour cream.

CALLALOO

Serves 6 to 8

Callaloo is a famed soup of the Caribbean Islands made with greens from aroid plants indigenous to that part of the world. Since callaloo greens are difficult to find outside of the Islands, a good substitute is Swiss chard, kale, or spinach, or, as in this recipe, a combination of all three. There are many variations of this soup, some of which call for pureeing the soup before adding the crabmeat and coconut milk, but I prefer the different textures.

½	pound red Swiss chard, stems and ribs removed
½	pound kale, stems and ribs removed
½	pound young spinach, stems removed
3	ounces salt pork, cut into ¼-inch cubes
2	garlic cloves, minced
1	medium onion, chopped
1	teaspoon fresh thyme leaves
5	whole scallions, white and green parts, coarsely chopped
¼	pound boiled or baked ham, cut into chunks
6½	cups Basic Chicken Broth (page 15)
	Vegetable oil (optional)
½	pound okra, stems removed, cut into ¼-inch rounds
1	Scotch bonnet pepper (habañero chile) or 5 red Thai peppers, seeded and finely chopped

½ **pound fresh cooked crabmeat**

½ **cup unsweetened coconut milk**

Salt

Tabasco sauce (optional)

4 **cups boiled white rice (optional)**

Wash the Swiss chard, kale, and spinach under running water. Dry on paper towels. Coarsely shred and set aside.

Fry the salt pork in a 4- or 6-quart heavy soup pot for 5 minutes over medium-high heat. Add the garlic, onion, and thyme. Sauté over medium-high heat until the pork is browned and crisp and the garlic and onion are soft and translucent, but not browned. Drain off and reserve any fat that may be left on the bottom of the pot. Add the Swiss chard, kale, spinach, scallions, and ham to the pot and lightly sauté 2 or 3 minutes. Pour in the broth, bring to almost a boil, lower the heat, and gently simmer, partially covered, 10 to 15 minutes.

Meanwhile, reheat the reserved fat in a nonstick skillet. It might be necessary to add a little extra vegetable oil. Sauté the okra and peppers, just until the okra is lightly browned and the peppers become aromatic. Scrape into the simmering soup, then add the crabmeat and coconut milk. Simmer 10 minutes, or until the okra is soft and the crab is heated through. Season with salt to taste and serve in a heated tureen or soup bowls, with Tabasco on the side if desired. If you prefer, add boiled rice to the tureen or ½ cup of rice to each bowl before adding the soup.

CHICKEN AND
SAUSAGE GUMBO

Serves 6 to 8

Almost a complete meal, this Louisiana dish is made with andouille sausage, but Polish kielbasa will work just as well.

4   pounds chicken breasts and thighs, cut into
        pieces
     Salt, freshly ground pepper, and cayenne
6   cups Basic Chicken Broth (page 15)
2   ounces bacon, diced
1   pound okra, sliced into ¼-inch rounds
     Olive oil (optional)
1   large onion, chopped
3   celery stalks, chopped
3   garlic cloves, minced
4   large tomatoes, peeled and chopped, or 1
        15-ounce can stewed tomatoes
1   large red bell pepper, seeded and chopped
1   pound andouille sausage, cut into 1-inch slices
1   small red chile, seeded and finely chopped, or
        crushed red pepper flakes to taste
     Roux (recipe follows)
½   pound uncooked shrimp, coarsely chopped
2½   cups hot cooked white rice
     Chopped scallions, green and white parts

Pat the chicken dry, then sprinkle with salt, pepper, and cayenne. Set aside. Add the broth to a large Dutch oven or pot, and bring to a slow simmer over medium-low heat.

Fry the bacon until crisp in a large cast iron skillet or Dutch oven. Remove and drain on paper towels, reserving the fat in the pan. Brown the chicken and okra on all sides in the bacon fat over medium-high heat. (If the pan isn't large enough, do this in batches.) Remove the okra as it lightly browns, and reserve. Continue cooking the chicken for 15 minutes, or until nicely browned on all sides. Drain on paper towels, then add to the simmering broth.

Pour off the excess fat from the skillet, and add a little olive oil if you prefer. Sauté the onion, celery, and garlic until soft and wilted. Add the tomatoes, red bell pepper, sausage, and chile and cook 5 more minutes. Add the roux, stirring constantly so the roux doesn't burn or over brown. Scrape the ingredients of the pan into the chicken broth and simmer about 30 minutes. Add the okra and shrimp and simmer 5 to 10 more minutes.

For easier eating, remove the chicken with tongs and let cool so you may remove and discard the skin and bones. Cut the chicken into bite-size pieces and return to the pot.

To serve, divide the cooked rice into individual bowls, ladle the gumbo over the rice, and sprinkle with scallions.

ROUX

True roux is made by adding all the flour at once and cooking it for 30 to 40 minutes to achieve a deep brown color. Here's an unorthodox method that is quicker.

¼ cup unsalted butter
¼ cup all-purpose flour

Melt butter in a pan over medium heat. Add the flour in small batches, whisking constantly as it browns. The roux will turn from tan to deep mahogany as it cooks. If the roux darkens too quickly, remove from the heat and keep stirring as it will continue cooking.

CHICKEN SOUP WITH CHICKPEAS AND COUSCOUS

Serves 4 to 6

Like a thick minestrone or a hearty stew, this soup tastes even better after being refrigerated for a day or two. For an exotic touch, stir the parsley into the soup just before serving, then dust the surface with a dash of ground allspice or cinnamon.

2½–3 pounds chicken pieces, washed and
trimmed of all fat
6 cups Basic Chicken Broth (page 15)
4 cups water
2 large onions, peeled
10 whole cloves
1 teaspoon black peppercorns

1   bay leaf
1   tablespoon olive oil
6   garlic cloves, chopped
3   large carrots, peeled and cut into ½-inch
      pieces
½   teaspoon turmeric
    Salt
3   cups cooked or drained and unrinsed
      canned chickpeas
1   cup medium-grain couscous
½   cup chopped fresh parsley
    White pepper

Place the chicken in a large Dutch oven or pot. Add the broth and water, partially cover, and bring to a simmer. Continue to skim the surface until clear. Add 1 onion, the cloves, peppercorns, and bay leaf. Simmer partially covered for 1 hour.

Remove the chicken from the pot and set aside to cool. Strain the soup and discard the onion, cloves, peppercorns, and bay leaf. Cool the soup, then skim the fat or chill overnight and skim.

Return the broth to the pot, and keep warm over low heat. Chop the remaining onion. Heat the oil in a large heavy skillet. Sauté the onion, garlic, and carrots over medium heat about 3 to 5 minutes, or until the onion is translucent. Scrape into the soup. Stir in the turmeric and season with salt to taste. Bring to an almost boil, lower the heat, and simmer, partially covered, for 15 to 20 minutes. Add the chickpeas and simmer for 5 minutes.

Meanwhile, cut the chicken from the bones. Discard the skin and bones. Shred or cut the meat into pieces, add to the pot, and simmer covered for 3 to 5 minutes. Remove from the heat and add the couscous. Cover and let sit for 3 to 5 minutes. Stir and adjust the salt and pepper to taste. Ladle the soup into bowls and sprinkle with parsley before serving. This soup thickens when refrigerated overnight, but thins out when reheated.

Variation: WITH ZUCCHINI Slice 3 or 4 medium zucchini into ¼-inch rounds. Proceed as above, adding the zucchini with the chickpeas. Cook about 10 minutes, or until the zucchini pieces are tender, then proceed as above. Omit the parsley and sprinkle with ½ cup freshly chopped basil.

PHO GA
(SPICED HANOI CHICKEN NOODLE SOUP)

Serves 4 to 6

This Vietnamese staple is usually made with spiced beef, but it is equally good with chicken. The Vietnamese eat this soup any time of the day—even for breakfast.

3½   **pounds chicken, cut into 8 pieces**

2   **pounds chicken wings or drummettes (meaty parts of the wing only)**

8   **cups Oriental Chicken Broth (page 16), or Basic Chicken Broth (page 15)**

> 3   scallions, green and white parts, trimmed
> ¼   pound gingerroot, peeled and cut into 3 pieces
> 3   tablespoons Asian fish sauce (*nuoc nam* or
>   *nam pla*)
> 3   whole star anise
> 1   teaspoon whole allspice
> 1   teaspoon black peppercorns
> 1   pound fresh rice vermicelli (*báhn pho*), or
>   ½ pound dry rice sticks (*maifun*)

GARNISH

> 1   cup bean sprouts, blanched for 2 to 3 seconds
> 1   bunch fresh cilantro, leaves only
> 1   bunch fresh basil, leaves shredded
> 1   bunch mint, leaves only
> 4   small red Asian chiles, minced
> 4   scallions, white part only, trimmed and
>   chopped
> 2   limes, cut into wedges

Wash the chicken under cold water and place in a large, heavy, deep soup pot that's not too wide. Add the broth. Bring to a simmer over medium-high heat, lower the heat, and simmer, uncovered, for about 30 minutes, skimming the scum as it rises to the top of the pot. Continue skimming until the soup is clear. Add more broth if necessary.

Add the scallions, gingerroot, fish sauce, star anise, allspice, and peppercorns. Simmer, partially covered, for 40 to 50 minutes.

Cool slightly, then remove the chicken. Remove the chicken from the bones and discard the skin and bones.

Cut the chicken into bite-size pieces, or shred, and set aside.

Strain the broth and discard the vegetables and spices. Skim the fat off the top of the soup with a large spoon, or use a gravy degreasing cup. (Or pour broth into a large bowl and chill overnight. The next day, remove the congealed fat from the surface before reheating the soup.)

Just before serving, return the broth and the chicken to the pot and bring to a simmer over medium heat.

Meanwhile, bring a large pot of water to boiling. Place a handful of vermicelli in a strainer, and rinse in running water. Dip the strainer full of noodles in the boiling water for 2 to 3 seconds. Repeat until all the noodles are used. Drain. If using dry rice sticks, rinse in cold water and cook in the boiling water for 1½ to 2 minutes, or until soft. Drain.

Place the noodles or rice sticks in individual soup bowls. Using a slotted spoon, top with a portion of chicken. Ladle hot soup into the bowls. Serve with garnishes arranged on a large platter and with a bowl of extra fish sauce on the side. Diners can add the garnishes along with a squeeze of lime and fish sauce to taste.

TUSCAN CHICKEN SOUP

Serves 4 to 6

The Swiss chard can be replaced with shredded Savoy cabbage and the rosemary with fresh thyme.

6	tablespoons olive oil
1	large onion, chopped
4	ounces pancetta or ham, chopped
1	pound Swiss chard, ribs and leaves, chopped
2	Roma (Italian plum) tomatoes, peeled, seeded, and chopped
2	cups cooked cannellini or other white beans
7	cups Basic Chicken Broth (page 15)
	Salt and freshly ground pepper
3	garlic cloves, crushed
1	small red chile
1	sprig fresh rosemary
1	cup grated Parmesan cheese

Heat 2 tablespoons of oil in a 4- or 5-quart heavy saucepan or Dutch oven. Sauté the onion and pancetta for 2 minutes over medium-high heat. Add the chard and stir quickly to wilt. Add tomatoes and beans. Sauté several minutes, then add the broth. Season with salt and pepper. Partially cover; simmer over low heat for 30 minutes.

Meanwhile, heat the remaining oil in a small pan. Brown the garlic with the chile and rosemary. Strain and pour the oil into the soup. Simmer 5 more minutes. Adjust seasonings and serve with grated cheese on the side.

DOUBLE MUSHROOM AND BARLEY CHICKEN SOUP

Serves 6

A huge bowl of hearty mushroom and barley soup is the consummate foil for a cold winter night. Try sautéing any combination of fresh, exotic mushrooms to vary the flavor and texture.

1	ounce dried black or shiitake mushrooms
1	tablespoon unsalted butter
2	tablespoons olive oil
1	large leek, trimmed leaving 2 inches of green, washed, split, and chopped (about 1½ cups)
1	small white onion, chopped
2	medium carrots, peeled and cut into ¼-inch rounds
½	cup pearl barley
8	cups Basic Chicken Broth (page 15)
½	pound fresh mushrooms, cleaned and sliced (about 3 cups)
2	tablespoons chopped parsley
	Salt and freshly ground white pepper
2	cups diced or shredded cooked chicken
3	tablespoons chopped fresh dill
	Crème Fraîche (page 93) or sour cream

Cover the dried mushrooms with hot water and soak for 20 minutes. When soft, pat dry with a paper towel, trim any tough ends, and coarsely chop. Reserve. Strain the soaking liquid into a small cup to remove any sand and set aside.

Heat the butter and 1 tablespoon of oil in a 4-quart Dutch oven or heavy saucepan. Sauté the leek and onion until soft and translucent. Add the reserved mushrooms, carrots, and barley. Sauté 2 minutes, stirring to coat evenly with the butter and oil, then add the chicken broth and the reserved mushroom liquid. Bring to just a boil, lower the heat, and simmer, covered, for 1 hour.

Meanwhile, in a large skillet, heat the remaining oil. Sauté the sliced mushrooms and parsley about 5 minutes, or until lightly browned. Season to taste with salt and pepper. After the soup has cooked 1 hour, add the sautéed mushrooms and the chicken. Adjust the salt and pepper, and cook 10 more minutes. If the soup is too thick, thin with a little broth, water, or milk.

Ladle the soup into bowls and garnish with dill and a dollop of Crème Fraîche or sour cream.

MULLIGATAWNY

Serves 6

Originating with the Tamils in the south of India as a thin, peppery vegetarian soup, Mulligatawny evolved into a thick, curried soup with meat favored by the British Raj. Some versions call for removing the chicken and bones, pureeing the soup, then returning the meat to the soup to reheat with a cup of yogurt. Cooked diced potatoes and cream are also a delicious addition for a more hearty soup.

2	pounds chicken thighs, skinned
¼	cup vegetable oil or unsalted butter
1	large onion, chopped
3	large celery stalks, sliced
4	large garlic cloves, finely chopped
1	tablespoon fresh gingerroot, finely chopped
1½	teaspoons cayenne
1	teaspoon ground coriander
1	teaspoon turmeric
1	large Granny Smith apple, peeled, cored, and cubed
3	Roma (Italian plum) tomatoes, peeled, seeded, and diced
2	large carrots, peeled and sliced
½	cup canned unsweetened coconut milk
6	cups Basic Chicken Broth (page 15)
½	cup dried red lentils, washed (see Note)

3   **tablespoons uncooked white rice**
4   **cups cooked basmati rice**

Cut the chicken from the bones and cut the meat into 1½-inch pieces. Reserve the bones.

Heat the oil or butter over high heat in a Dutch oven or large heavy pot. Sauté the onion and celery for 3 to 4 minutes, or until the onion is translucent. Stir in the garlic, gingerroot, cayenne, coriander, and turmeric and cook 1 or 2 minutes to blend the flavors. Add the chicken meat and bones; sauté about 2 minutes, stirring to brown evenly. Add the apple, tomatoes, and carrots and sauté about 5 minutes, stirring occasionally. Stir in the coconut milk and cook about 5 minutes, then pour in the chicken broth and lentils. Stir to evenly distribute the ingredients. Lower the heat and simmer, covered, for ½ hour. Add the uncooked rice, cover, and cook for 15 minutes more.

Before serving, remove and discard the chicken bones. Put about ⅓ cup of the basmati rice in each serving bowl. Ladle the soup over the rice. Or, if you wish, you can prepare the rice separately and serve it on the side.

Note: Red lentils can be found in health-food stores and Middle Eastern markets, as well as in the ethnic food sections of large supermarkets. They turn pale pink when cooked and have a more delicate flavor than green or brown lentils, which also take longer to cook.

AJIACO
(CHICKEN AND POTATO SOUP)

Serves 6

Some versions of this Colombian soup call for mashing the potatoes in the pot. Here, the creamy texture is complemented by chunks of disintegrating potatoes.

1	4-pound chicken, cut into 8 pieces
8	cups Basic Chicken Broth (page 15)
3	small white onions, sliced
2	leeks, white part only, cleaned and split
2	large carrots, peeled and cut into chunks
1	bay leaf
½	teaspoon ground cumin
	Salt and freshly ground pepper
2½	pounds red, russet, and yellow Finnish potatoes, peeled and cut into ¼-inch slices
3	medium ears white corn, cut into 2-inch pieces

CONDIMENTS

1	cup chopped fresh cilantro
½	cup sliced scallions, green and white parts
6	tablespoons capers, rinsed
1	cup Crema Mexicana (page 33) or heavy cream
3	limes, cut into wedges
2	avocados, peeled, cut into wedges, and sprinkled with lemon juice

Wash the chicken under cold running water. Place in a heavy 5- or 6-quart Dutch oven or casserole. Add the broth and bring to a simmer over medium-high heat. Lower the heat and simmer, uncovered, for about 30 minutes, skimming the scum as it rises to the top. Continue skimming until the soup is clear. You might need to add a cup or 2 of water if too much liquid has evaporated.

Add the onions, leeks, carrots, bay leaf, cumin, and salt and pepper to taste. Gently simmer, partially covered, for 1 hour, or until the chicken is tender.

Remove the chicken from the pot and let cool. Remove the chicken from the bones, and discard the skin and bones. Cut the chicken into bite-size pieces and set aside.

Strain the broth, reserve the vegetables, and discard the bay leaf. Skim any fat off the top of the broth. (Or pour broth into a large bowl and chill overnight. The next day remove the congealed fat from the surface before reheating the broth.)

Return the broth to the pot, bring to simmering over medium-high heat, and add the potatoes. Lower the heat, cover, and cook about 30 minutes, or until the potatoes are very soft and falling apart. Add the corn, the reserved chicken, leeks, onions, and carrots. Simmer, covered, about 5 minutes, or until the corn is cooked and everything is heated through. Adjust the salt and pepper to taste.

Place the cilantro, scallions, capers, Crema Mexicana, lime wedges, and avocado in small individual bowls.

Ladle the soup into serving bowls. Top each with the condiments and a squeeze of lime juice.

ESCAROLE, SUN-DRIED TOMATO, AND BASMATI RICE CHICKEN SOUP

Serves 6

Charles Saunders, the chef-owner of the Eastside Oyster Bar and Grill in Sonoma, California, and a good friend, created this flavorful and healthy soup especially for this book.

2	tablespoons olive oil
½	cup chopped yellow onion
1	teaspoon chopped garlic
½	cup basmati rice
	Pinch of saffron threads, or ¼ teaspoon saffron powder
1¼	cups water
6	cups Basic Chicken Broth (page 15)
4	chicken drumsticks or thighs
½	cup sun-dried tomatoes, cut into medium dice
2	cups escarole leaves, trimmed, washed, and coarsely chopped

GREMOLATA

¼	cup finely chopped fresh parsley
1	tablespoon finely chopped fresh thyme leaves
1	teaspoon finely chopped lemon zest
½	teaspoon finely chopped garlic

Heat the oil in a large saucepan, add the onion and garlic, and sauté over medium-high heat until the onion is translucent. Add the rice, saffron, and water. Bring to a boil, lower the heat, cover, and cook for 30 minutes or until the rice is tender.

Meanwhile, add the broth and chicken to a large pot. Partially cover and cook over medium-low heat, skimming as necessary, until the chicken is tender, about 30 to 40 minutes. Remove the chicken from the broth. When the chicken is cool enough to handle, remove the meat from the bones and discard the skin and bones. Shred the chicken into long strips and set aside.

Add the tomatoes to the broth and allow them to reconstitute for 3 to 4 minutes. Add the rice mixture, chicken, and escarole. Heat to just simmering. Just before serving, mix all the Gremolata ingredients and stir into the soup.

Variation: EGG FLOWER SOUP For a delicate Oriental-type soup, proceed as above. Just before serving, add 2 lightly beaten egg whites to the hot soup in a slow, steady stream. Swirl to lightly cook and shred the egg whites, then ladle the soup into bowls. Serve with or without the Gremolata.

Ann Wilder's
Cambodian Hot Pot

Serves 6

This main-course soup, based on a recipe from friend Ann Wilder of Vann's Spices in Baltimore, is a lighter version of the traditional Mongolian hot pot made with thinly sliced beef. The soup is cooked in a chimneyed hot pot, available wherever Chinese cooking utensils are sold, but a chafing dish, electric frying pan, fondue pot, or even a Chinese chimney steamer can also be used.

¼	pound cellophane noodles
6	cups Basic Chicken Broth (page 15)
1	1-inch piece of fresh gingerroot, peeled and thinly sliced
3	whole star anise pods
3–4	stalks fresh lemon grass, cut into 1-inch pieces, or ½ cup dried lemon grass
2	cups unsweetened coconut milk
1	tablespoon chopped fresh cilantro
3	garlic cloves, minced
1	tablespoon freshly grated gingerroot
2	tablespoons dark Oriental sesame oil
2	tablespoons rice wine or dry sherry
½	cup light soy sauce
1	pound boneless and skinless chicken breasts, cut into bite-size pieces
1	pound sea scallops

1	pound medium shrimp, peeled and deveined
½	pound snow peas
1	small head bok choy, tough leaves discarded, washed and cut into bite-size pieces
8	scallions, trimmed and halved
8	fresh water chestnuts, peeled and cut into thin slices, or 1 can water chestnuts
6	ounces fresh shiitake or button mushrooms, quartered

Soak the noodles in 2 cups of water for 30 minutes. Drain and cut the noodles into 6-inch pieces. Set aside.

Meanwhile, in a medium pot, combine the broth, sliced gingerroot, star anise, and lemon grass. Simmer over medium heat, covered, for 20 minutes. Strain, and discard the gingerroot, star anise, and lemon grass.

Just before serving, combine the broth with the coconut milk, cilantro, garlic, and grated gingerroot in a chimneyed hot pot. Place over low heat and bring to a simmer.

Meanwhile, make a dipping sauce by combining the sesame oil, rice wine, and soy sauce in a small bowl. Divide equally among 6 bowls.

Arrange the remaining ingredients, including the reserved noodles, on a platter near the pot. Let each diner select the meat and vegetables of his or her choice to cook, and place in the simmering liquid. Cover the pot and cook until you hear the liquid boiling. Remove the lid.

Each diner can spoon out his or her selection to eat with the dipping sauce as a first course. Keep the broth hot and serve it as a second course in the dipping bowls.

ELEGANT
CREAM SOUPS

GOLDEN CHICKEN AND SWEET PLANTAIN SOPA

Serves 4 to 6

My good friend Norman Van Aken is one of the great chefs of Miami Beach. He's known for his imaginative cooking style that combines the flavors of Key West, Cuba, and the Caribbean. He created this soup especially for this book during one of his cooking classes. Annatto seeds (or achiote) can be purchased at Latin American grocery stores. You may wish to garnish the soup further with a dollop of sour cream and a few thinly sliced, crisp fried plantain chips.

2	teaspoons ground cumin
1	teaspoon freshly ground pepper
	Salt
2	large skinless and boneless chicken breasts
¼	cup Annatto Oil (recipe follows)
1	large, very ripe plantain, peeled and cut into ½-inch-thick slices
	Pinch of salt
	Pinch of sugar
	Pinch of cayenne
¼	cup olive oil
2	tablespoons unsalted butter
1	cup finely diced leeks, white part only

½	cup finely chopped red onion
½	cup finely chopped celery
½	cup finely chopped carrots
3	garlic cloves, sliced
2	Scotch bonnet peppers (habañero chiles), stemmed and seeded
	Pinch of saffron
1	bunch fresh cilantro leaves, washed, dried, and finely chopped
1	cup freshly squeezed and strained orange juice
4½	cups Basic Chicken Broth (page 15)
2	cups half-and-half or cream (see Note)

Heat a small skillet. When a drop of water sizzles on the bottom of the pan, add the cumin and pepper and toast about 1 minute. Let cool and combine with salt to taste. Sprinkle the mixture on both sides of the chicken. Place the chicken on a plate and drizzle with the annatto oil, turning the chicken several times to coat. Cover and chill for at least 1 hour, to allow the oil to deeply color the chicken.

Meanwhile, sprinkle the plantain slices with a pinch of salt, sugar, and cayenne. Place a large heavy pot or Dutch oven over medium-high heat. When the pan is hot, add the olive oil and butter. Sauté the plantains until golden on both sides. Add the leeks, onion, celery, carrots, garlic, and chiles. Stir, and cook until the vegetables are soft and lightly browned. If necessary, add a small amount of oil to the pan. Add the saffron, cilantro, and orange juice. Stir in the chicken broth. Lower the heat and simmer 10 to 12 minutes, stirring often. Pour the soup in small batches into a blender or food processor and puree until smooth. Return to the pot, add the half-and-half or cream, and adjust seasoning. Set aside.

Place the chicken in a nonstick skillet and sauté over medium heat about 3 minutes per side, or until just cooked through. Remove, cool slightly, and cut into bite-size pieces.

Gently reheat the soup until it's warm but not boiling and ladle into warm bowls. Garnish with the chicken and serve.

Note: To prepare the soup without the half-and-half or cream, thoroughly stir in two pureed or mashed plantains for a more substantial texture.

ANNATTO OIL

Makes 2 cups

¼ **cup annatto seeds**
2 **cups olive oil**

Place the annatto seeds in a dry skillet and toast over medium heat for 30 seconds. Gradually add the olive oil and slowly cook for 3 to 4 minutes. Remove from the heat and allow to steep about for 30 minutes. Strain and discard the seeds. Pour the oil into a bottle or jar and store tightly closed in a cool place out of the sunlight.

TOM KA KAI
(CHICKEN AND COCONUT MILK SOUP)

Serves 4

This is well worth a trip to a Thai or gourmet market for authenticity's sake. *Galangal* (also known as *laos* and *ka*) is a root that's a little less pungent than ginger.

2⅓	cups canned coconut milk (19-ounce can)
1	cup Basic Chicken Broth (page 15)
2	large chicken breasts, or ¼ chicken, boned, skinned, and cut into bite-size pieces
2	stalks lemon grass, cut into 1-inch pieces
2	kaffir lime leaves, or 2 strips lime peel
1	3-inch piece *galangal*, or fresh gingerroot
3	serrano or Thai chiles, seeded and minced
1½	tablespoons *nam pla* (Thai fish sauce)
	Juice of 1 lime
2	scallions, green and white parts, finely sliced
4	fresh cilantro sprigs, leaves only

In a medium saucepan, bring the coconut milk and broth to a boil. Add the chicken, lemon grass, kaffir lime leaves, and *galangal* or ginger. Simmer, partially covered, for 15 minutes, or until the chicken is tender.

Remove from the heat. Strain out the lemon grass, lime leaves, and *galangal*. Stir in the chiles and reheat to simmering. Before serving, stir in the *nam pla* and lime juice. Ladle the soup into individual bowls and sprinkle with scallions and cilantro.

AVGOLEMONO

Serves 4 to 6

This thick and creamy soup from Greece is delicious hot or cold, but shouldn't be reheated once chilled.

- 6 cups **Basic Chicken Broth (page 15)**
- ⅓ cup **short-grain rice, such as Arborio**
- 4 large **egg yolks**
  - **Strained juice of 3 lemons (about ⅓ cup)**
  - **Salt and freshly ground white pepper or cayenne**
  - **Chopped parsley**
  - **Snipped chives**
  - **Thin lemon slices (optional)**

In a medium saucepan, bring the broth to just boiling. Add the rice, partially cover, lower the heat, and simmer for 15 to 20 minutes, or until the rice is tender. Remove from heat.

Meanwhile, place the egg yolks and lemon juice in a small bowl and whisk until frothy. When the rice is cooked, remove 1 cup of the hot broth and slowly pour it in a stream into the egg mixture, whisking constantly. Slowly whisk the mixture into the soup pot, whisking constantly to prevent curdling. Reheat over very low heat, stirring constantly with a wooden spoon, for 2 to 3 minutes. Season with salt and pepper or cayenne to taste. Ladle into warm bowls and garnish with parsley, chives, and lemon slices. Serve immediately.

Pureed Cream of Chicken Soup

Serves 6 to 8

Arborio rice and Crème Fraîche create a creamed soup with a lot less fat than one enriched with cream and eggs. Use the combination as a base to create any variety of creamed vegetable soups.

 8 cups Basic Chicken Broth (page 15)
 1 large skinned and boned chicken breast, halved
 2 tablespoons unsalted butter
 1 teaspoon canola oil
 1½ cups chopped leek (white part only), or yellow onion
 ½ cup Arborio or any short-grain rice
 ¼–½ cup Crème Fraîche (page 93)
 ⅛ teaspoon ground nutmeg
 Salt to taste
 Pinch of cayenne
 Snipped chives

In a small pot or shallow pan, bring 2 cups of the broth and 1 cup of water to a boil. Remove from the heat. Add the chicken. Cover pot and let stand for 20 minutes.

Meanwhile, heat the butter and oil in a medium (3- to 4-quart) pot or saucepan. Add the leek or onion and sauté over medium heat 3 to 4 minutes, or until translucent. Add the rice and stir to coat each grain with the oil. Add 4 cups of broth. Bring to just boiling over high heat, stirring occasionally to keep the rice from sticking to the bottom of the pan. Lower the heat and simmer, partially covered, for 20 minutes, or until the rice is soft.

Puree the mixture in 1½-cup batches in a blender until very smooth. Return the puree to the saucepan.

Remove the chicken from the cooking pot and discard the liquid. Cut the chicken into small cubes.

Pour the remaining chicken broth into the puree and stir to combine well. Remove 1 cup of the mixture and combine with the Crème Fraîche. Whisk the mixture back into the soup, then whisk in the nutmeg and salt and cayenne to taste. Add the cubed chicken. Heat the soup over very low heat, stirring constantly so it doesn't stick to the bottom of the pan. Ladle into bowls and garnish with chives.

Variation: CHICKEN AND CORN SOUP Prepare the soup as above, replacing the nutmeg with 1 teaspoon ground thyme or cumin. Before adding the cubed chicken to the soup, puree 2 cups of fresh or defrosted frozen yellow or white corn in a blender until smooth. Set aside. Sauté 1 cup of chopped yellow onion and ½ cup chopped celery in 1 tablespoon butter and 1 tablespoon corn oil in a skillet until the onions are pale golden. Add 2 additional cups of fresh or frozen corn to the skillet and sauté 2 minutes. Add the pureed corn, cooked vegetables, and chicken to the soup. Heat through. Adjust seasonings. Serve with roasted red pepper strips or chopped scallions for garnish.

Note: For a thicker soup, reduce the broth by 1 or 2 cups.

SENEGALESE SOUP

Serves 4

Traditionally a creamed curried soup, this low-fat version uses cooked vegetables to thicken the broth instead of cream and egg yolks.

- 3 tablespoons unsalted butter
- 3 stalks celery, leaves removed, chopped (about 1 cup)
- 1 large onion, chopped (about 2 cups)
- 1 tablespoon curry powder
- 6 cups Basic Chicken Broth (page 15)
- 2 tart green apples, peeled, cored, and coarsely chopped
- 1 cup diced cooked chicken,
- 4 teaspoons chopped fresh chives

Melt the butter in a heavy 4-quart saucepan or pot, and add the celery and onion. Sauté over medium-high heat until the celery wilts and the onions are translucent but not brown. Lower the heat and add the curry powder. Cook for 5 minutes, stirring occasionally.

Add the broth and apples. Partially cover, and simmer over medium-low heat for 35 to 40 minutes, or until all the vegetables are very soft.

Strain the broth and degrease if necessary. Reserve the vegetables. Add a little broth to a blender, then add a portion of the vegetables. Puree the vegetables until they are very smooth. Repeat, until all the vegetables are pureed.

Combine the strained broth and puree, stirring to blend well. Return the soup to a saucepan, add the chicken, and slowly reheat. Ladle into bowls and garnish with chives. To serve cold, chill the soup and chicken in the refrigerator for several hours and mix in the chicken just before serving.

CUMIN-SCENTED CREAM OF SWEET POTATO SOUP

Serves 4

Sweet potatoes are often called either garnet or jewel yams. For this soup, use the garnet yams, which are the moist orange sweet potatoes with deep red skin.

2	tablespoons corn or canola oil
2	large leeks, white part only, cleaned, split, and chopped
4	garlic cloves, minced
2	shallots, chopped
½	teaspoon ground cumin
1	pound sweet potatoes, peeled and cut into ½-inch chunks
1	large carrot, peeled and cut into ¼-inch slices
3½–4½	cups Basic Chicken Broth (page 15)
⅓	cup plus 4 teaspoons half-and-half
¼	cup Crème Fraîche (page 93)
	Salt and freshly ground white pepper
3	jalapeño or serrano chiles, seeded and minced

Heat the oil in a large pot. Add the leeks, garlic, shallots, and cumin. Sauté over medium-low heat for 1 minute. Lower the heat, cover, and cook for 10 minutes, or until vegetables are soft and translucent, stirring occasionally. Add the sweet potatoes, carrot, and 3½ cups broth. Raise the heat and bring to a quick boil, then lower the heat, partially cover, and simmer, stirring occasionally, for 25 to 30 minutes. Cool for 5 minutes. Pour into a strainer, reserving the liquid. Transfer the vegetables to a food processor or blender, and puree until smooth. Slowly pour the reserved liquid through the feed tube and continue pureeing until the mixture is very smooth.

Return the soup to the pot and stir in ⅓ cup of the half-and-half and the remaining chicken broth. If a thinner soup is desired, thin with additional broth.

Thin the Crème Fraîche with the remaining half-and-half. Set aside. Slowly reheat the soup to almost a simmer, stirring often to make sure it doesn't stick to the bottom of the pot. Season to taste with salt and pepper. Ladle into warm bowls, drizzle a little Crème Fraîche over the soup, and sprinkle with jalapeños.

CREAM OF SUGAR PUMPKIN SOUP

Serves 4 to 6

If the smaller and sweeter sugar pumpkins are not available, use a small regular pumpkin.

3	tablespoons unsalted butter
2	medium onions, sliced
1	large carrot, scraped and coarsely chopped
1½–2	pounds fresh sugar pumpkin pulp, cut into 1-inch chunks
4	cups hot Basic Chicken Broth (page 15)
1	cup half-and-half
½	teaspoon ground ginger
¼	teaspoon ground mace
½	teaspoon freshly ground white pepper
	Fresh chives, chopped

Melt the butter in a medium pot. Add the onions and carrot and cook over low heat until the onions are wilted and translucent. Add the pumpkin and hot broth.

Cook for 10 minutes, or until the pumpkin is tender. Remove from the heat and, in small batches, puree the mixture in a food processor or blender, pouring the puree back into the pot as it's processed.

Add the half-and-half, ginger, mace, pepper, and salt to taste. Reheat over medium-low heat, until just boiling.

Top with chives and serve immediately.

CHILLED AVOCADO SOUP WITH RED PEPPERS AND CAVIAR

Serves 6

Serve this elegant soup, based on a recipe from chef Barbara Figueroa, for a special-occasion dinner.

2½ cups Basic Chicken Broth (page 15)
1½ cups half-and-half
4 large, very ripe avocados (Haas preferred)
1 tablespoon fresh lemon juice
3 tablespoons minced red onion
   Salt and freshly ground white pepper
⅓ cup finely diced roasted, skinned, and seeded
      red bell pepper (about 1 medium pepper)
      (see page 35 for roasting directions)
6 ounces any high-quality black caviar

Combine the broth and half-and-half. Heat in a double boiler over simmering water until well blended and warm. Do not boil. Remove and cool to room temperature.

Puree the avocados with the lemon juice and 1 table-spoon of the minced red onion. Transfer to a nonreactive mixing bowl. Stir in the cooled broth. Season to taste with salt and pepper. Chill several hours until completely cool. Ladle into chilled cups and sprinkle each with the remaining onion, red peppers, and caviar. Serve immediately.

ACCOMPANIMENTS
AND CONDIMENTS

TURKEY WONTONS

Makes about 65 wontons

You can vary the fillings by using ground chicken, or a combination of ground pork and turkey, chicken, or veal. Finely chopped water chestnuts, carrots, or celery are also good additions.

1	tablespoon vegetable oil
1	pound ground turkey
1	cup finely chopped Napa (Chinese) cabbage
2	tablespoons finely chopped cilantro leaves
2	scallions, white and green parts, finely chopped (about ¼ cup)
1½	teaspoons finely minced fresh gingerroot
2½	teaspoons dark Oriental sesame oil
1	tablespoon cornstarch
1	large egg, lightly beaten
1	tablespoon light soy sauce
1	1-pound package prepared wonton skins

Heat the oil in a nonstick skillet over high heat until very hot. Add the turkey and brown well over medium-high heat. Drain off any fat. Transfer the turkey to a food processor, add the cabbage, cilantro, half the scallions, and the gingerroot, and process just until the mixture is finely chopped. Turn into a bowl and stir in the sesame oil.

Combine the cornstarch with 1 tablespoon of water to make a paste, then mix into the egg. Thoroughly combine with the turkey mixture. Return the mixture to the skillet and cook over medium heat for 5 minutes, or until thickened and not wet. Remove from the heat and stir in the soy sauce and remaining chopped scallions.

To make the wontons, place the wonton wrapper, with a corner point toward you, on a cutting board or other work surface. Place 1 teaspoon of the turkey mixture in the upper center of the wrapper. With a small pastry brush or your finger, moisten the two top edges of the wrapper. Fold the wrapper in half to form a triangle, pinching or pressing the edges firmly together. Place a dab of water on the three points of the triangle. Fold the right corner up to meet the top point. Fold the left corner up, over the right corner. Press with two fingers to tightly seal. Place on a cookie sheet lightly dusted with cornstarch. Repeat with remaining wontons. (At this point, you can freeze the wontons and defrost later as needed. Frozen wontons can be cooked in boiling water.)

Before cooking, place a cookie sheet or roasting pan next to the stove and fill about ¼-inch deep with a little chicken stock or warm water.

Bring a large pot of water to a boil. Cook the wontons, in batches without crowding, for 5 minutes, or until they float to the top. Remove with a slotted spoon, and place on the cookie sheet or in the pan until ready to serve. They can remain at room temperature for 1 hour. Otherwise, refrigerate in the pan until ready to serve.

Variation: STEAMED WONTONS First, sauté the wontons in batches of 10 or 12. For each batch, heat about 1 tablespoon of oil in a 12-inch skillet. Place the wontons in the pan and sauté over medium-high heat about 1 minute, or until lightly browned on one side. Add just enough water to cover to about ¼-inch depth (about ⅔ cup). Cover, lower the heat, and steam for 5 minutes. Uncover, and cook another minute or two, until all the water is absorbed. Serve with dipping sauce or in soup.

EGG BARLEY
(FARFEL)

Serves 4 to 6

Egg barley, or farfel, is made from egg noodle dough that is grated before being dried and cooked.

⅔ **cup all-purpose flour**
1 **large egg, slightly beaten**
¼ **teaspoon salt**

Combine the flour, egg, and salt either by hand or in a food processor until the dough is sticky but holds together. Roll into a ball, then knead on a lightly floured surface to form a stiff ball. If necessary, add flour while kneading.

Cut the dough in half and roll into narrow logs. Let the dough dry until stiff enough to grate. Grate on the coarsest side of a cheese grater. Spread out on a towel-covered cookie sheet and let dry completely.

If not using immediately, store in a glass jar at room temperature, or freeze in an airtight container.

Cook the farfel in lightly salted boiling water about 10 minutes, then drain and add to soup.

FLUFFY KASHA

Makes 3 cups

Kasha (buckwheat groats) has a delicious sweet and
nutty flavor and is commonly added to chicken soup by
Jewish cooks from Eastern Europe.

> 2 cups Basic Chicken Broth (page 15)
> 2 tablespoons Rendered Chicken Fat (*schmaltz*)
>   (page 92), unsalted butter, or vegetable oil
> 1 cup kasha
> 1 large egg, slightly beaten

In a medium saucepan, heat the broth and chicken fat to
a simmer. Cover, and keep hot over very low heat.

Meanwhile, in a bowl stir the kasha into the beaten egg,
making sure each grain is coated with egg. Place in a 1½-
or 2-quart ungreased heavy saucepan or skillet. Toast over
medium heat, stirring constantly with a wooden spoon,
until each grain is dry and separate, about 3 minutes.

Remove the pan from the heat and carefully pour the
hot soup over the kasha. The soup may splatter when
pouring. Cover the pan or pot tightly, and place over medium-low heat. Steam 10 minutes. Uncover and stir, check-
ing if all the liquid has been absorbed. If not, cover and
cook an additional 3 to 5 minutes. Remove from the heat
and fluff with a fork. Serve ½ cup of kasha per bowl.

Variation: KASHA VARNISHKES   In a heavy saucepan,
sauté 1 cup of chopped onions in the chicken fat, butter, or

vegetable oil until translucent. Pour the broth into the pan, heat to simmering, and proceed with the above recipe. Meanwhile, cook 8 ounces of egg pasta bowties (*farfalle*) or shells according to package directions. When the kasha is cooked, toss with the hot, drained pasta and 1 tablespoon of butter or *schmaltz*. Season with salt and pepper. Serves 6 as a side dish, or add the Kasha Varnishkes to soup.

PESTO

Makes about 1 cup

Pesto makes a wonderful flavoring for soups. I prefer to float a teaspoon on top of the soup without stirring it in, which can give the soup a muddy appearance.

2 cups fresh basil leaves, tightly packed
½ cup pine nuts
¼ cup freshly grated Parmesan cheese
3 garlic cloves
½ cup extra-virgin olive oil
1 tablespoon unsalted butter, softened
Salt (optional)

In a food processor, puree the basil, pine nuts, cheese, and garlic. Slowly add the oil to make a thick paste. Stir in the butter and season to taste with salt. If not using immediately, scrape into a jar or plastic container with a lid and pour a thin layer of olive oil on top. It will keep in the refrigerator for several weeks, or it can be frozen for several months. Thaw and stir before using.

CUSTARD ROYALE

Serves 6

Tasty, decorative shapes of custard can transform a plain cup of chicken broth into an elegant first course. Before baking, flavor the custard with a sprinkling of your favorite chopped fresh herbs or spices, or with a tablespoon of roasted garlic or roasted red pepper puree, or a combination of both.

> 1½ **teaspoons unsalted butter**
> 3 **large egg yolks**
> 1 **large egg**
> ½ **cup heavy cream**
> ½ **cup Basic Chicken Broth (page 15)**
> ¼ **teaspoon salt**
> **Pinch of ground nutmeg**

Preheat the oven to 325° F. Butter an 8-inch square Pyrex pan.

In a medium bowl, beat together the egg yolks and egg. Slowly whisk in the cream and broth, blending thoroughly. Skim off any foam. Pour the mixture through a fine mesh strainer into the prepared pan.

Place in a larger pan filled with enough hot water to come halfway up the sides of the baking dish. (This will ensure slow, even cooking and a creamy-textured custard.) Bake for 35 to 40 minutes, or until the custard is firm.

Let cool, then refrigerate until well chilled. Cut the custard into 1-inch strips and carefully remove the strips with a long, narrow spatula. Cut each strip into small decorative shapes with an aspic cutter or sharp knife. Bring to room temperature on a plate before adding to hot soup.

FARINA DUMPLINGS

Makes about 20 dumplings

Light, fluffy, and irregularly shaped, farina dumplings are a favorite soup addition in Hungarian cooking.

- 2 **tablespoons unsalted butter, at room temperature**
- 1 **large egg, slightly beaten**
- 5 **tablespoons regular farina, such as Cream of Wheat**
  Pinch of salt
- 9 **cups Basic Chicken Broth (page 15)**

Cream the butter, then beat in the egg, farina, and salt. Refrigerate 10 to 15 minutes.

Meanwhile, bring the chicken broth to a gentle boil in a large pot. Remove the dumpling mixture from the refrigerator and drop by ½ teaspoonfuls into the broth. Lower the heat to a simmer, cover, and cook the dumplings for 15 minutes. Turn off the heat and let the dumplings rest for 5 minutes before serving with the soup. Serve immediately.

Note: Dumplings can be prepared in soup or water early in the day or a day in advance.

RENDERED
CHICKEN FAT
(SCHMALTZ)

Makes about 2 cups

A small amount of rendered chicken fat, used to enhance the flavor of certain foods such as matzo balls, adds a rich, chickeny taste far superior to that imparted by oil. *Schmaltz* was probably originally used as a convenient butter replacement by Old World cooks, particularly those who followed kosher dietary laws that forbid the mixing of dairy and meat at the same meal.

Collect any trimmed fat or fatty skin from uncooked chickens and store in airtight containers in the freezer until you have about 1 pound. The rendered fat will keep almost indefinitely in the refrigerator.

1   **pound chicken fat and fatty skin, diced**
1   **yellow onion, diced**
2   **slices unpeeled apple**

Place the fat and skin in a heavy pan. Slowly cook over low heat until the fat is almost melted. Add the onion and apple slices and continue cooking until the onions are browned and the skin cracklings (*grebenes*) are crisp.

Cool the fat, strain into a clean, dry glass jar, cover tightly, and refrigerate. Discard the apple slices. The onions and cracklings can be stored separately in the refrigerator. Use them as a topping for crackers or crusty bread, or to flavor a variety of dishes from egg salad to chopped liver.

Note: Rendered chicken fat can also be purchased in the Jewish food section of the supermarket or even at a kosher poultry market.

CRÈME FRAÎCHE

Makes 2 cups

Homemade crème fraîche will keep about two weeks in the refrigerator. It's the perfect addition to soups and sauces because it doesn't curdle when boiled. For an elegant soup topping, whip it slightly and float a dollop on your favorite soup.

> 2 cups heavy cream, preferably not ultra-
>   pasteurized, at room temperature
> ½ cup sour cream

Pour the heavy cream into a stainless steel bowl or large glass measuring cup. In a smaller cup or bowl, thin the sour cream with a little of the cream, then stir into the remaining cream. Pour the mixture into a clean glass jar, and cover loosely. Let it thicken to the consistency of thin sour cream at room temperature for anywhere from 4 to 12 hours, depending on the warmth of the room. Cover the jar tightly and refrigerate. The crème fraîche will thicken to the consistency of sour cream when thoroughly chilled.

ACKNOWLEDGMENTS

First and foremost I have to thank my mother, Jean Zimmerman, who taught me how to make great chicken soup and who, eventually, learned and taught me how to make equally good matzo balls.

As always, there would be no book without my editor, Shirley Wohl, and her assistant Ellis Whitman; and my agent Barbara Lowenstein and all her staff, especially Norman Kurz.

I'm particularly indebted to my husband, Gerry Goffin, whose support and criticism during the final stages of this book made the writing easier and more pleasurable.

The following friends were great tasters and wonderfully generous with their ideas and recipes during the writing of this book: Helen Bercovitz, Linda Burum, Suzanne Dunaway, Susan Fine and Michael Moore, Rochelle Huppin and Cathleen Venezia of Chefwear, Phyllis Lerman, Bobby, Josh, and Tory Littman, Michael Maron, Joe Patti, Ellen Rose and the Cook's Library, Geri Wilson, and Trudy and Ernest Zingg.

A special thanks to those whose recipes or versions thereof are in this book: Ann Wilder and chefs Barbara Figueroa, Joe Venezia, Charles Saunders, Stephen Pyles, "Henry Clay" Richardson, and Norman Van Aken.

Finally, thanks to Kevin Lowery and the Campbell Soup Company for their generosity. They contributed a wealth of information and an unlimited supply of Swanson's Chicken Consomme, which I used to successfully retest the recipes I originally made with homemade broth.